from the album eric clapton unplugged

by Wolf Marshall

ISBN 0-7935-8792-1

7777 W. BLUEMOUND RD. P.O. BOX 13819 MILWAUKEE, WI 53213

Visit Hal Leonard Online at
www.halleonard.com

eric clapton
from the album eric clapton unplugged

CONTENTS

INTRODUCTION

MTV's Unplugged sessions established a highly popular venue where artists would perform purely, or at least mainly, acoustic sets. The program presented a number of diverse performers over the years from legends like Paul McCartney, Bruce Springsteen, and Rod Stewart to blues masters such as Stevie Ray Vaughan and hard rock bands Nirvana, Aerosmith, Tesla, and Kiss. Eric Clapton, who had been an acoustic performer throughout his career, was an obvious Unplugged candidate. For his offering, he recorded a remarkable two-hour set at Bray Studios near Windsor in England on January 16, 1992. The personnel consisted of Eric and his old friend Andy Fairweather Low on guitar, bassist Nathan East, Steve Ferrone on drums with Ray Cooper supplying extra percussion, and Chuck Leavell on keyboards. Additionally, Katie Kissoon and Tessa Niles contributed sympathetic backing vocals. Interestingly, Clapton had initial reservations about releasing the *Unplugged* record, feeling it would only appeal to a niche market. He was pleasantly surprised less than a year later when it became his biggest selling album to date, resulting in a glorious sweep at the Grammy Award ceremonies.

Eric Clapton Unplugged remains a high water mark in the genre. In retrospect, it was a remarkably diverse outing exploring the full range of Clapton's artistry in acoustic form. Included in the program were authentic rural blues, dramatic rock ballads, dixieland, bossa nova, earthy folk songs, and more—all delivered with Eric's uncategorizable but immediately recognizable guitar style.

This special signature licks presentation is offered as a guitarist's companion book/audio to the *Eric Clapton Unplugged* album. The music/TAB displays note-for-note transcribed guitar parts, and is accompanied by text and performance notes explaining points of interest and various technical aspects of the music. The CD audio features authentic play-along band tracks in stereo split (the featured guitar part is isolated on the right side, accompaniment is on the left side)—so that you may try your hand at the music in context—as well as detailed demonstrations of the techniques and licks discussed in the book. The latter are broken down into bite-sized phrases and played slowly.

For the motivated student, it would be helpful to have the following additional materials.

The video: *Eric Clapton Unplugged.* Warner Reprise video #38311–3.
The audio: *Eric Clapton Unplugged.* Reprise Records W2–45024
The songbook: *Eric Clapton Unplugged.* Guitar Recorded Versions. Hal Leonard Corp. #HL00694869

THE RECORDING

Wolf Marshall: guitars & mandolin, percussion
Mike Sandberg: drums & percussion
Michael Della Gala: bass
John Nau: keyboards
Michael McCarty: additional percussion on "Tears in Heaven" and "Layla"
Nils Johnson: fretless bass on "Tears in Heaven"
Ray Kenetsky: keyboards on "Layla" and "Tears in Heaven"

Recorded at Pacifica Studios, Los Angeles, CA, and Marshall Arts Studios, Malibu, CA.

Produced by Wolf Marshall

Special thanks to Todd Wright at Dobro/Gibson USA, Keith Brawley and Bill Cummiskey at Fender Musical Instruments, and Mike Pinter at Thomastik-Infeld strings.

Extra special thanks to Dick Boak and Chris Martin at The Martin Guitar Company.

AN UNPLUGGED AXOLOGY

| Martin Acoustic | Dobro | Nylon-String Acoustic | 12-String Acoustic |

The Martin 000-28EC Eric Clapton Signature model was created in 1996 in collaboration with the man himself. Its unique design is based on a combination of features and dimensions uniting the two specific vintage Martins that Eric favors in the studio and on stage—a vintage 1939 000-42 and a vintage 000-28. Both are classic 000 small-bodied acoustic guitars, though the 000-28 was modified by inlay artist/historian Mike Longworth with a style 45 fingerboard, headstock, and top pearl. These instruments were made highly visible in the MTV Unplugged concert and on the Grammy-winning CD. The 000-28EC has the smaller 000 body with scalloped braces and short 24.9" scale length—popular among blues and fingerstyle guitarists—which produce a delicate, airy, and balanced tone (more common jumbos and dreadnoughts tend to accentuate the bass frequencies). Handcrafted of select solid woods throughout, the back and sides are East Indian rosewood and the top is bookmatched from quartersawn Sitka spruce. The ebony fingerboard features 1 3⁄4" nut width, and pre-war Style 28 snowflake markers in abalone pearl with Eric Clapton's signature inlaid between the nineteenth and twentieth frets. Other noteworthy aspects include a modified V-Shape neck, vintage-style "butterbean" open-geared tuning keys, and an older Martin logo decal on the headstock. The Martin 000-28EC is featured prominently on this Signature Licks recording, notably on "Layla," "Hey Hey," and on all the solo steel-string demos. It was strung with medium-light gauge Martin SP3100 bronze strings which further enhanced its distinctive tone.

Also notable was the Dobro F60 Classic guitar used on "Running on Faith," "Walkin' Blues" and "Rollin' and Tumblin'." This is similar to the model Clapton played in concert, with a slotted headstock and a metal resonator plate on a wood body—differing only in the ornamentation and use of F-holes instead of round meshed soundholes. For more details see "Running on Faith." The Dobro line is currently available through Gibson USA. A Jim Dunlop heavy glass slide (#211) was used for the slide parts. "Signe," "Lonely Stranger," and "Tears in Heaven" were played on a Fender nylon-string acoustic, model CG 25SCE. The acoustic 12-string used on "Alberta" and "San Francisco Bay Blues" was a Fender DG-31-12. These instruments were strung with Thomastik-Infeld Plectrum, Spectrum series bronze, and Classic C nylon strings. Some compression and limiting were applied at the board via a Symetrix 528 mike processor. All of the aforementioned acoustics were recorded with an AKG C1000S condenser microphone.

SIGNE

By Eric Clapton

Figure 1 – Intro and Theme

"Signe" is one of several songs Eric Clapton composed while mourning the death of his son Conor and healing himself. Composed in 1992, on a beautiful yacht of the same name, it was the first piece Clapton wrote in his healing process. On *Unplugged,* "Signe" is played as an ensemble tune and begins the concert. Eric and second guitarist Andy Fairweather Low render the samba-style instrumental on nylon-string acoustic guitars. Appropriately, they employ a fingerstyle plucking approach which has its roots in Brazilian bossa nova music of the sixties—as does the syncopation which is prevalent throughout the rhythm figures. Both aspects contribute to "Signe's" light jazz feel.

Eric Clapton uses his customary three-fingers-and-thumb technique to pluck chords and single notes. Note that he does not position his hand in the traditional classical posture. Instead of the standard arched-wrist position, he favors a *collapsed wrist* approach which rests on the strings near or on the bridge, facilitating muting and anchoring. This is essentially an adaptation of Clapton's electric-guitar fingerpicking technique.

The head of "Signe" employs simple extended chord voicings, such as minor sevenths and dominant sevenths with suspended fourths, in the thematic A–B/A–E/G♯ changes. The chord progression of D/F♯–E7sus4–E7 was clearly a recurring thematic idea in Clapton's writing of the period, and also appears prominently in "Tears in Heaven."

3 Featured Guitars:
Gtr. 1   meas. 1-24

4 Slow Demos:
Gtr. 1   meas. 1-7;
            8-12; 13-16;
            17-20

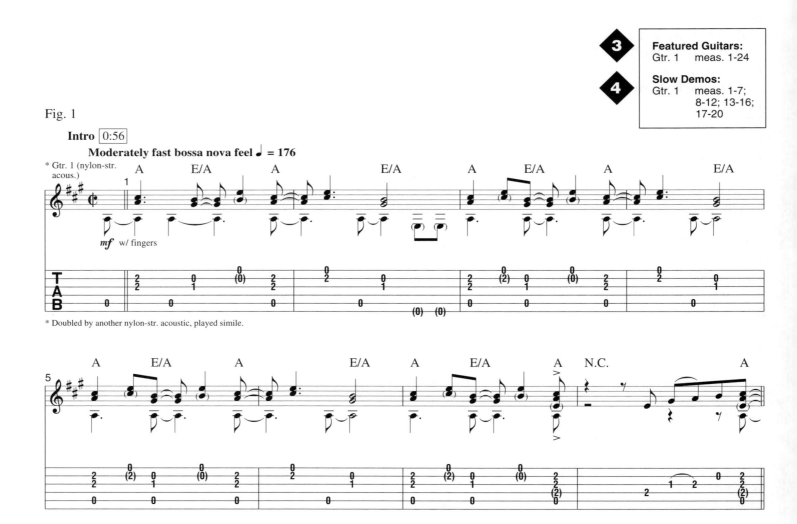

Fig. 1

Intro 0:56

Moderately fast bossa nova feel ♩ = 176

* Gtr. 1 (nylon-str. acous.)

mf w/ fingers

* Doubled by another nylon-str. acoustic, played simile.

Figure 2 – Bridge

The feel in the bridge (1:51) is more driving and rhythmic. Here accents and space are purposefully exploited for a strong result. The sound is more dynamic and "pianistic" with "claw-style" fingerplucking used by both guitarists. The hammered-on B/C♯–C♯m7 figure in measures 1 and 5 is crucial and calls for a bit of practice to acquire the necessary technique. Begin by building your left-hand strength and precision by playing a clean, buzz-free index barre at the fourth position. Then, focus on adding the E and G♯ notes with the second and third fingers while maintaining the barred shape below. Also noteworthy are the characteristic samba-based syncopations as well as the jazzy *cycle-of-fifths* progression of C♯m7–F♯m7–Bm7–A/B–E.

Fig. 2

Featured Guitars:
Gtr. 1   meas. 1-20

Slow Demos:
Gtr. 1   meas. 1-4;
           9-12

* Doubled by another nylon-str. gtr., played simile.

BEFORE YOU ACCUSE ME (TAKE A LOOK AT YOURSELF)

Words and Music by Eugene McDaniels

Figure 3 – Intro and Verse

"Before You Accuse Me" looks back to Eric's early musical beginnings. In fact, this was very likely one of the first records he ever heard. A solid Bo Diddley composition, it is a straight 12-bar blues in E—allowing Clapton maximum space for reinterpretation. He had played the tune as an electric number in concert for years, and recorded it that way on 1989's *Journeyman*. In 1992, it found its way into the *Unplugged* set as an attractive two-guitar arrangement.

Eric and second guitarist Andy Fairweather Low approach "Before You Accuse Me" as a moderate shuffle on twin steel-string flat-top acoustics. Their fingerstyle articulation is eclectic and somewhat random, combining fingerplucking and fingertip strumming—as on the E7 triad in measure 15. In the verses, Clapton's part is the straighter of the two and assumes a rhythm guitar role, comprised mainly of root-fifth to root-sixth blues comping. Andy's playing provides color and contrast in the form of subtle lead fills and single-note counterlines.

7 Featured Guitars:
Gtr. 1   meas. 1-16

8 Slow Demos:
Gtr. 1   meas. 1-4;
           5-8; 9-13;
           13-16

Fig. 3

* Key signature denotes E Mixolydian.   ** On track 7, this half measure is played simile.

Figure 4 – Outro Guitar Solo

Eric's ending solo (3:04) is a high point of the *Unplugged* session, and an engrossing study of his blues improvising approach. He begins with double stops implying the E7 chord of the progression in measures 1–3 followed by a bluesy single-note lick in E minor pentatonic (E–G–A–B–D) in measure 4. Over the A7 chord in measures 5, 6, and 10, Clapton uses a hybrid scale which is a familiar blues-guitar concept. Here, he adds the C♯ note (the major 3rd of A) to the E blues scale (E–G–A–B♭–B–D), purposely accentuating the chromatic effect of the B–B♭–A melody line. In measures 7 and 8, Eric plays lower-register blues licks based on the E Mixolydian mode (E–F♯–G♯–A–B–C♯–D). Note the mix of triad and single-note textures and the inclusion of the G note in measure 7 and in the trill figure of measure 8. The B7 chord in measure 9 is a country blues staple; it is arpeggiated and allowed to ring for full duration. Clapton ends the song with bent double stops which have been an E.C. signature lick since "Ramblin' on My Mind" on *Blues Breakers.* The final cadence employs the ascending progression of D♯9–E9, a standard blues closer, for a solid and authoritative result.

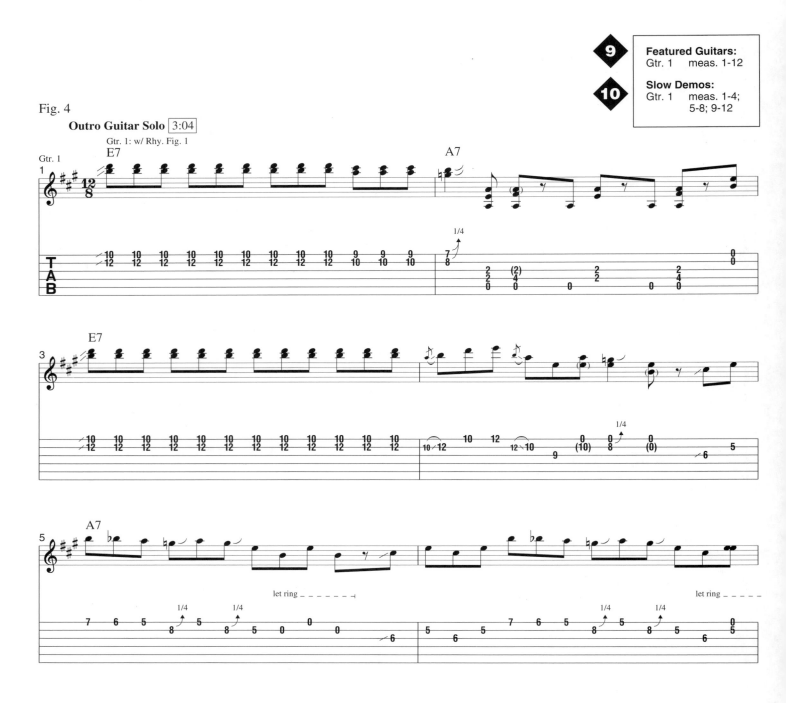

Fig. 4

Outro Guitar Solo 3:04

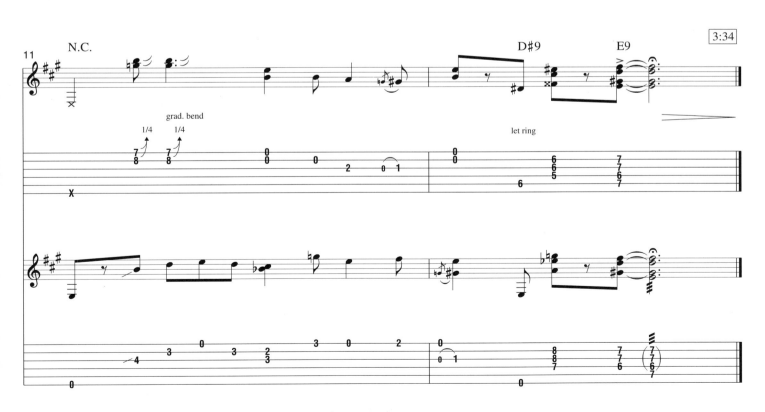

HEY HEY
Words and Music by William "Big Bill" Broonzy

Figure 5 – Intro (Main Theme)

More than half of the tracks on *Unplugged* are reinterpreted blues standards—loving tributes to Eric's seminal influences. One of the most compelling is his rendition of William "Big Bill" Broonzy's "Hey Hey." This song recalls Clapton's earliest repertoire, and is another of the tunes he originally played as a youth in the British folk club circuit of the early sixties. According to Eric he never mastered it, so he "gave it another shot" on *Unplugged.*

"Hey Hey" is a straight 12-bar, blues in E—like "Before You Accuse Me." Similarly, Clapton plays it fingerstyle on steel-string acoustic with his usual thumb-and-three-fingers approach—openly acknowledging the Delta blues school. The allusions to the genre in the intro figures (and main theme) are inescapable. Note the quarter-step double-stop bends on the E7#9 chord, as well as the regularly pulsing bass-note thumps on the I and IV chord portions (E7 and A7) of the progression in measures 1–8. The ideas found in the last four measures of the 12-bar progression are also staples of the country blues vernacular. Note the use of B7 as a partial-barre chord in measure 9, and a memorable melodic figure over A7 and E combining fretted notes and open strings in measures 10 and 11. The latter is a strong and recurrent central riff throughout "Hey Hey."

11 Featured Guitars:
Gtr. 1 meas. 1-12

12 Slow Demos:
Gtr. 1 meas. 1-4;
5-8; 9-12

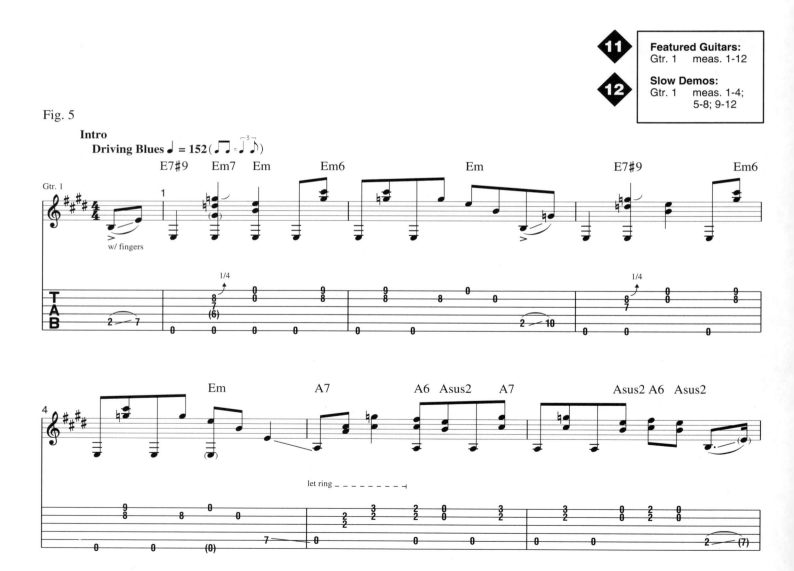

Fig. 5

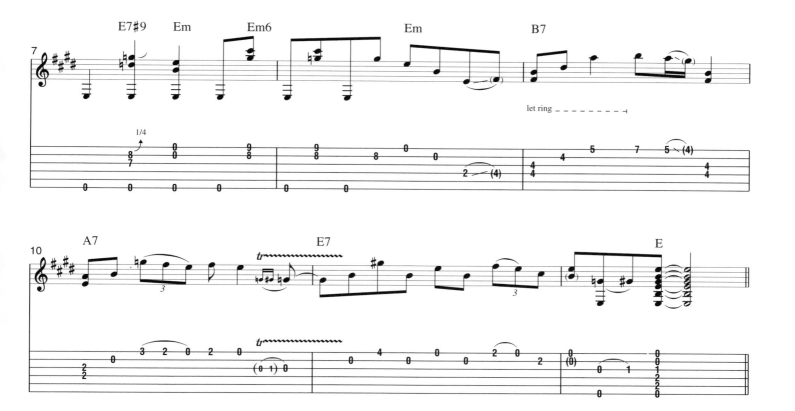

Figure 6 – Verse

The verses in "Hey Hey" are marked by a strong shuffle feel. Note the heavy emphasis on the pulse in Clapton's comping with the steady bass notes of measures 1–3 and 5. These are picked with the thumb and are placed below the upper partial chords which are generally picked with the fingers. The figures in measures 4 and 7–8 present a secondary riff in the song. These are based on the E7 chord form in the first position, and use the lifting off and fretting of the D note (with the pinky on the second string) as an important aspect of the melody pattern. The sounds in measures 9–12 are variants of the B7–A7–E licks found in the main theme.

13 Featured Guitars:
Gtr. 1   meas. 1-12

14 Slow Demos:
Gtr. 1   meas. 1-4;
          5-8; 9-12

Fig. 6

TEARS IN HEAVEN

Words and Music by Eric Clapton and Will Jennings

Figure 7 – Intro, Verse, and Chorus

The gigantic hit, "Tears In Heaven," a haunting tribute to Clapton's late son Conor, first appeared in the film *Rush,* and was later included in the *Unplugged* collection. Clapton plays it on nylon-string acoustic with a quasi-classical fingerpicking style (which has a warm and intimate quality) and allows for a variety of articulation and arpeggiation options. The approach enables him to pluck selected tones or chords to create fuller chord sounds, thinner dyads, or purely single-note passages at will, resulting in a beautiful, multi-textured accompaniment. Andy Fairweather Low (Gtr. 1) takes an active role in the song adding decorative fills during the verses. The chord sequence of D/F#–E7sus4–E7–A in measures 3–4 was previously heard in "Signe," and was evidently a pervasive compositional idea during this phase of Clapton's writing. Note the signature thumb fretting technique used to play the sixth string bass notes in the E/G#–F#m–D/F# chords of the progression.

For the main thematic riff in the intro and verse, Eric employs a number of simple first-position chords (A, D, and E) decorated with tasty embellishments in the form of hammer-ons, pull-offs, and slides. These elements are present in the accompaniment pattern used during the bulk of the arrangement.

The chorus is more active harmonically, with broader chordal texture in Clapton's part than in the previous sections—relying on a consistent alternating thumb-and-fingers picking pattern. The chords are broken up with a regular bass note/upper partial pattern until the phrase rejoins the main thematic riff in measure 19. In the chorus, Low (Gtr. 1) adds a complementary, harp-like arpeggiated figure as a varied accompaniment.

Fig. 7

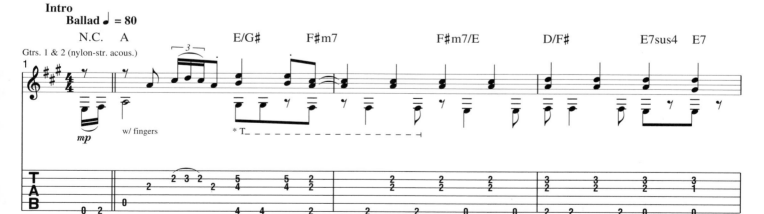

Figure 8 – Bridge and Interlude

In the bridge, Eric modulates to a somewhat remote key—G major—for an interesting, expressive musical effect. He alludes to a piece of the main riff's chord progression in the similar C–G/B–Am sequence (transposed)—maintaining a tight thematic unity within the composition. Clapton varies his fingerpicking approach to include more chordal arpeggiation textures.

17 Featured Guitars:
Gtr. 2   meas. 1-16

18 Slow Demos:
Gtr. 2   meas. 1-4;
          5-8; 9-12

Fig. 8

LONELY STRANGER
Words and Music by Eric Clapton

Figure 9 – Intro

"Lonely Stranger" is also from Eric's "healing process" song cycle. He wrote the song in Los Angeles during the *Rush* filmscore project to cheer himself up. It is a slow, lilting but restrained number with hints of gospel and pop styles, featuring strong but sympathetic accompaniment from the band. This arrangement again finds Clapton on nylon-string acoustic with Fairweather Low adding thoughtful and colorful touches on mandolin.

Clapton begins the song with an improvised solo blues guitar intro. This brief excursion is played with the fingers and employs the familiar scale-combining approach endemic to his style. Throughout, his lines alternate between major and minor modality—mixing notes from both the E Mixolydian mode (E–F♯–G♯–A–B–C♯–D) and the E minor pentatonic scale (E–G–A–B–D). Check out the rolling ostinato figure in measure 5. This beloved blues cliché is right out of the T-Bone Walker songbook. The ensuing bent double stops lead directly to the song's main riff.

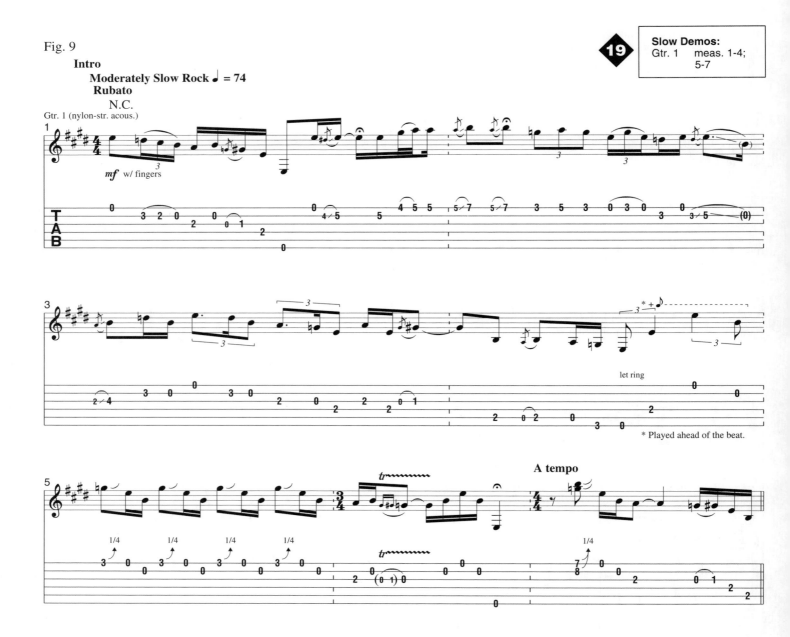

Fig. 9

Slow Demos:
Gtr. 1   meas. 1-4;
5-7

Figure 10 – Intro and Verse

The song's main riff is a strong chordal figure introduced at 0:19, immediately after Eric's opening licks. It is based on an E–A–Am6–E progression and occurs over a constant low E pedal point. The *thumb slap* in the riff (generally on beat four of the figure) is played by striking the guitar body just over the bass strings. It is a variant of the *flamenco golpe* technique and adds a nice percussive touch to the rhythm figure. Adapting his individualistic fingerstyle approach, E.C. establishes a pattern of bass note-chord-dyad-chord-bass note-thumb slap in the riff—essentially a steady eighth-note pattern. Notice the emphasized syncopation on the and-of-two throughout. The song's verses and chorus utilize similar articulations with different chord progressions.

20 Featured Guitars:
Gtr. 1 meas. 1-19

21 Slow Demos:
Gtr. 1 meas. 1-2;
9-12; 13-15

Fig. 10

* slap thumb on gtr. top.

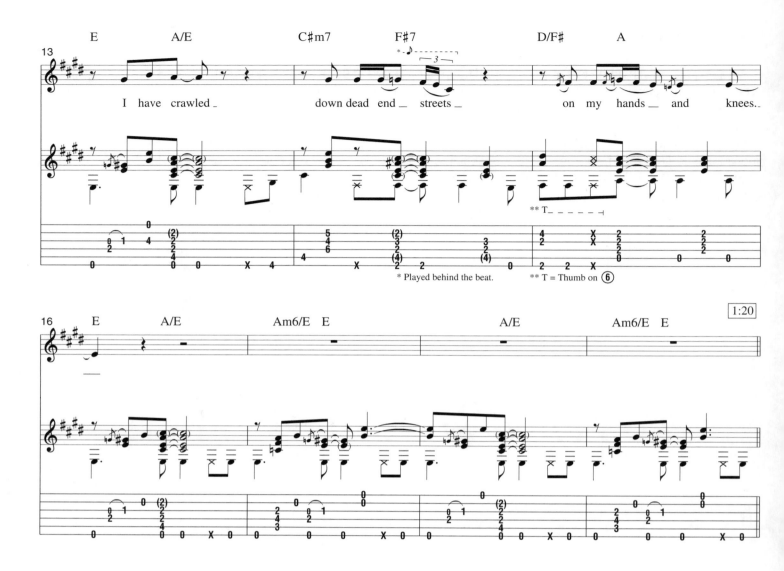

Figure 11 – Chorus

The chorus (at 1:40) accentuates the underlying gospel mood of the song particularly in the A–A#dim–E/B–C#m7–F#7–B9 chord progression of the second phrase (measures 5–7). Clapton closes the chorus by restating the song's main theme.

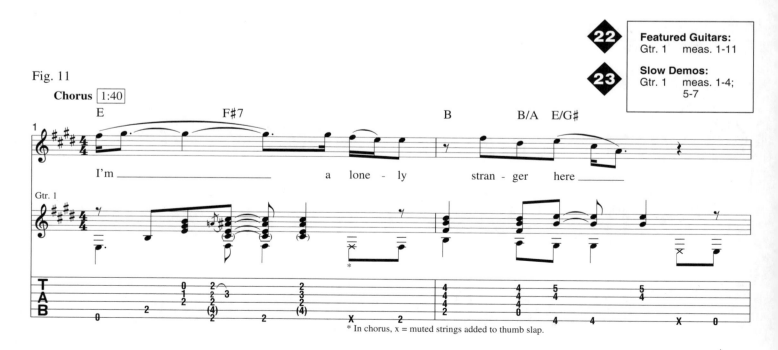

Fig. 11

Chorus 1:40

22 **Featured Guitars:**
Gtr. 1   meas. 1-11

23 **Slow Demos:**
Gtr. 1   meas. 1-4;
5-7

* In chorus, x = muted strings added to thumb slap.

* Thumb slap only.

NOBODY KNOWS YOU WHEN YOU'RE DOWN AND OUT

Words and Music by Jimmie Cox

Figure 12 – Intro and Verse

Unplugged was the ideal setting for "Nobody Knows You When You're Down and Out." This hardy, blues-tinged number from Bessie Smith goes back to around 1910 or 1915. It recalls Eric's earliest influences, and was also part of his repertoire in the clubs and pubs of his youth. The song was originally recorded by Clapton as a hard-edged, blues-rock number on the classic *Layla* album of 1970, and has remained a perennial favorite ever since. This version features a shuffling, barrel house feel with both Eric and Andy on steel-string flat-top acoustic guitars.

Clapton begins the song establishing a simple, fingerstyle pattern in the first four measures which forms the basis for the entire tune. His approach is a modified "stride-piano-meets-Travis picking" style in which the thumb and fingers separate bass notes from plucked partial chords. In the music all downstemmed notes are to be played with the thumb while the upstemmed chords are plucked with the fingers. The basic progression uses both I, IV, and V chords (C, F, and G) as well as more colorful *secondary dominants* (E7, A7, and D7). Open chords make up the first phrase (measures 1–4): C–E7–A7–Dm–A7–Dm. The second phrase (measures 4–8) combines first-position triads (F and F# diminished) with chromatic bass lines (ascending and descending) and open chords (C, A7, D7, and G7). Note the thumb-fretting technique on the D7/F# chord in measure 7. The eight-measure intro progression is also the verse progression.

24 Featured Guitars:
Gtr. 1   meas. 1-16

25 Slow Demos:
Gtr. 1   meas. 1-4;
5-8

Fig. 12

Intro

Moderately slow shuffle ♩ = 90

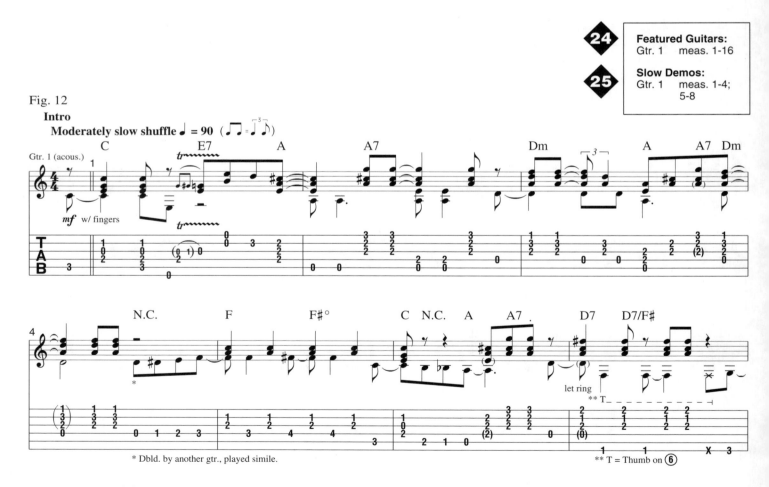

* Dbld. by another gtr., played simile.

** T = Thumb on ⑥

Figure 13 – Guitar Solo

This brief gem of a solo (1:46) is only eight measures long but speaks volumes. Clapton plays this predominantly single-note statement with a flat pick which he grabs moments before the solo. The highlights are numerous and noteworthy. He begins with a loping C major pentatonic (C–D–E–G–A) line over the C–E7–A7 chords in measures 1 and 2. Note the ending notes, C♯ and A, which clearly define the A7 chord, and reveal that Eric is quite aware of the harmonic twists and turns of the progression. This is further strengthened in measures 3 and 4, where his lines spell out the D minor tonal center. Note the use of the ninth (E) and a strong chromatic melody (C–C♯–D) in the phrase.

Clapton plays the A blues scale (A–C–D–E♭–E–G) over the F and F♯dim chords in measure 5, which is a crafty way of mixing basic blues-guitar sounds with more extended harmonic relationships. The descending chromatic minor thirds in measure 6 reinforce this effect and again emphatically outline the C–A7 chord progression. Eric's closing thoughts include slurred double-stop sixth intervals in measure 7 and a final rising chromatic melody in measure 8. These are also harmonically-based ideas and further indicate his strong note-to-chord improvisational strategy in the solo.

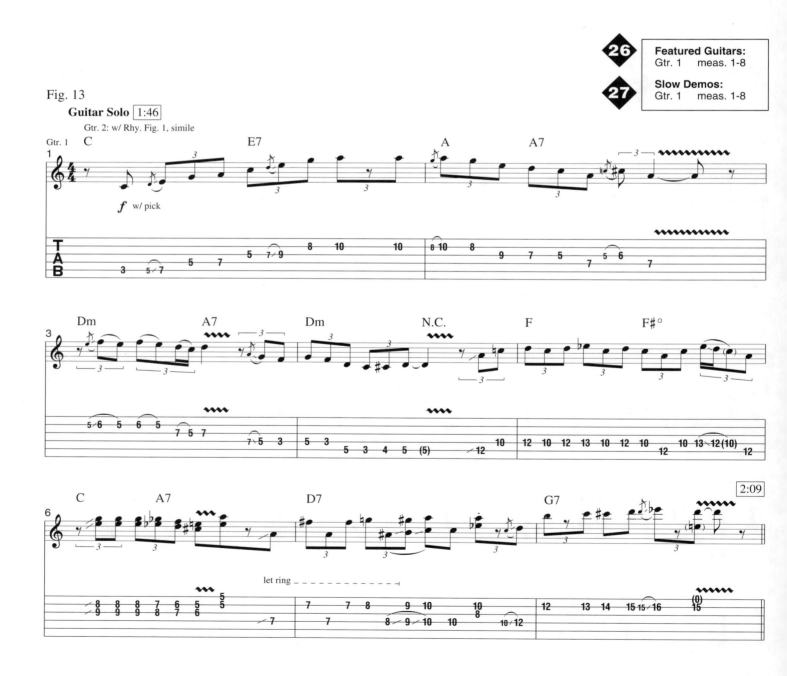

26 Featured Guitars: Gtr. 1 meas. 1-8

27 Slow Demos: Gtr. 1 meas. 1-8

Fig. 13

Guitar Solo 1:46

LAYLA

Words and Music by Eric Clapton and Jim Gordon

Figure 14 – Intro, Verse, and Chorus

Eric introduced "Layla" with the challenge, "Let's see if you can spot this one." His "jazzier" arrangement, with its slow shuffle groove and acoustic setting, might have confounded a few for a short time, but judging from the audience response to the opening measures, you can't hide a riff and a song as strong and memorable as "Layla" for long—no matter how it's disguised. On the track, Clapton plays his flat-top steel-string acoustic with a pick while Andy Fairweather Low lays down a solid rhythm part on a gorgeous old Gibson Super-400 arch-top acoustic.

The intro to the new "Layla" is begun as a solo by Eric and embodies the song's familiar progression in the changes of Dm–B♭–C. You could call this an "acousticized" version of the original classic chord riff. It is also heard in measures 21–28 as the central rhythmic figure of the chorus. Clapton plays a tasty single-note intro solo in measures 6–12, which is unmistakable with its sensitive blues-rock phrasing, characteristic finger vibrato, and D minor pentatonic (D–F–G–A–C) melody lines. Note the inclusion of the ninth (E) which produces a six-note "hexatonic" scale (D–E–F–G–A–C) throughout his improvisations—another trademark Slowhand trait.

The verse is contrastingly fluid and modulatory. It moves to the unrelated key of C♯ minor and proceeds through a series of chords that never quite seem to fully resolve. Clapton approaches this section with a different strummed articulation which latches on to the background groove and contributes to a more propulsive rhythmic feel.

28 Featured Guitars:
Gtr. 1   meas. 1-28

29 Slow Demos:
Gtr. 1   meas. 1-4;
6-12; 13-16;
17-20

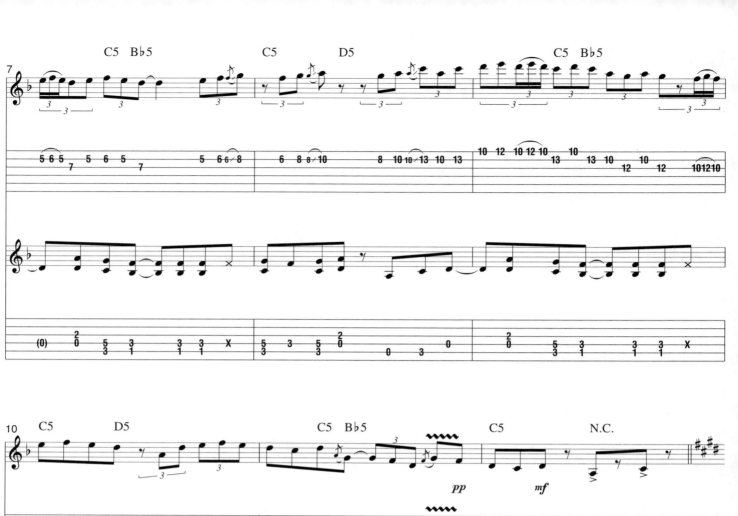

Verse

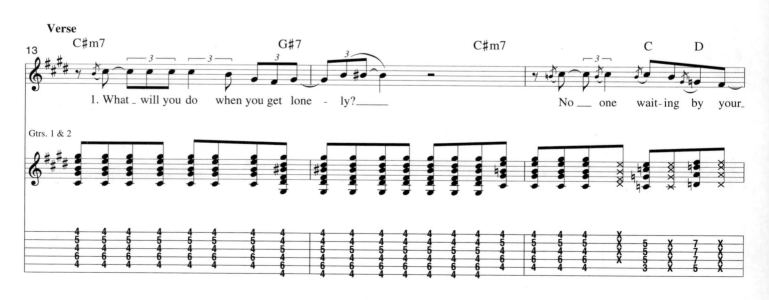

1. What will you do when you get lone - ly? No one wait-ing by your

Figure 15 – Guitar Solo

Eric's guitar solo is also played with a flat pick, and contains many of the signature melodic and rhythmic elements of his style. It strikes a perfect balance between outright blues improvisation and song conscious rock and pop, mixed with just a subtle hint of swing jazz—implied largely in the rhythmic placement of licks and their triplet-based feel. He immediately develops a nice pace in the solo, digging in solidly with bent double-stop blues riffs in the first measure. Slurred double stops are exploited in measures 3 and 4. Clapton relaxes a bit with a loping, single-note D minor (hexatonic) melody in measure 5.

Check out the amalgam of ideas in the solo's climax in measures 9-12. Eric begins an aggressive bent lick on beat two, then imitates it two measures later—a familiar swing jazz device combined with a timeless blues guitar mannerism. He closes the solo with D minor pentatonic and blues lines that combines single-notes with chords and double-stop textures.

Fig. 15

Guitar Solo

Featured Guitars:
Gtr. 1   meas. 1-16

Slow Demos:
Gtr. 1   meas. 1-8;
9-16

RUNNING ON FAITH

Words and Music by Jerry Williams

Figure 16 – Intro and Verse

Unplugged features a great version of "Running on Faith," a track first heard on 1989's *Journeyman.* Written by Jerry Lynn Williams, it was part of Clapton's regular stage repertoire, and an obvious choice for inclusion in the set. Like the original recording, "Running on Faith" features Eric on a *Dobro* resophonic guitar playing sultry country-blues slide licks. Ideally suited for the piece, this instrument has a unique timbre and a fluid, echoing voice which immediately evokes images of the Delta and country blues. Its sound and appearance necessitates some basic explanations for the uninitiated. Essentially, it is a wood-bodied, flat-top acoustic guitar with a dish-shaped resonator plate mounted on its face. The bridge of the guitar is seated on a spider whose eight legs rest on a delicate, resonating cone under the plate which amplifies the string vibrations and produces its distinctive tone. Eric's Dobro has small, mesh-covered soundholes on the upper bout while others have stylized F-holes similar to those on the National Style O model resophonic guitar. As generic as Coke or Thermos is in industry, the Dobro is now a given in the guitar world for this musical application. "Running on Faith" affords us a rare opportunity to examine Clapton's live Dobro work as he usually does not play it in his regular concerts.

Eric tunes his Dobro to *Open G tuning.* This is a slack tuning created by lowering the sixth (E), fifth (A), and first (E) strings one whole step each to D, G, and D respectively. This procedure generates a G major chord in open strings (from low to high): D–G–D–G–B–D. The open tuning is extremely advantageous and facilitates chordal sounds produced by the straight slide bar. Clapton exploits the natural chord tendencies of this tuning in many of his solo licks and fills throughout the song.

Most of Eric's playing in "Running on Faith" is done with the *slide.* He wears a glass slide (also called bottleneck) on his pinky and appears to use very little left-hand muting. It appears that most of the muting comes from the right hand wrist, palm, and fingers. As with all slide playing, the slide surface rests on the string *over the frets* just enough to make solid contact for strong, clean notes, and is never pressed toward the fingerboard as in normal fretting. In the song, Clapton plucks and strums the notes and chords with a flat pick.

The intro sets the tone for the song. Eric's opening single-note licks have a gently weeping quality accentuated by the slurred delivery and vocal vibrato of the slide playing. His intro lines in measures 1–4 are primarily based on the G major pentatonic scale (G–A–B–D–E). The F note in measure 4 defines the G7 chord and sets up a strong chord-based approach in measures 5–8. Note the use of arpeggio melodies for the C and D chords in this section, as well as three and four-note chords played with the slide. The chromatic melody line in measure 8 (D–Db–C) is a recurring theme in the song. Eric's chord-melody fills in the verse are essentially variations of his opening licks.

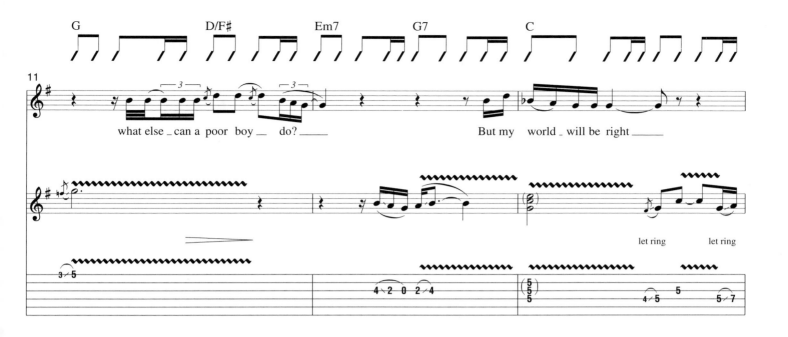

Figure 17 – Guitar Solo and Bridge

Eric's eight-measure slide solo is a highlight of the *Unplugged* session. His lines are melodious and song-conscious, and largely make use of the G major pentatonic scale (G–A–B–D–E). Chord shapes are exploited for the C and D chords of the progression in measures 4–6. These licks have a distinct country sound emphasized by the chromatic lead-in notes of the phrase.

Eric's closing ideas are based on a contrastingly bluesy two-measure phrase in the G Mixolydian mode (G–A–B–C–D–E–F). Note the A#/Bb tone used to emphasize the major third (B) by approaching it as a slide from a half step below. This is a classic blues and country technique found in much of Clapton's bottleneck work during the set.

Figure 18 – Outro Guitar Solo

The outro is more aggressive, blues-oriented, and rhythmically active. It occurs over a repeating vamp of G–F–C, which implies the G Mixolydian mode and provides strong harmonic contrast to the more diatonic changes of the verses. Eric digs in with edgy slide licks based on triad and chord shapes found at the twelfth, tenth, and fifth positions. Note that the B♭ major chord (seen as part of the G minor pentatonic scale) at the third fret is incorporated in many of the C sections to add a deeper blues quality. The blues quality is further emphasized in the climbing G minor pentatonic line of measure 5. In measures 6 and 10, Clapton plays familiar blues ostinato riffs over the C chord. Though these are G major triads, they function beautifully over the IV chord.

In the closing measures (13–16), Eric plays fingered chords on the Dobro. Note the interesting F6 and Cadd9 voicings created by forming normal chord shapes in the open tuning. His final thoughts in measures 18–20 are played in free time and consist of blues-based slide licks in the third and first position. These again combine G Mixolydian and G minor pentatonic melody and, in the quirky manner of country blues, end on an unresolved IV chord (C).

Fig. 18

37 **Featured Guitars:**
Gtr. 1   meas. 1-20

38 **Slow Demos:**
Gtr. 1   meas. 1-12;
13-14; 18-20

Guitar Solo 4:58

Love   comes   o - ver   you.

Gtr. 1

f

steady gliss.   *steady gliss.*

* Played behind the beat.

Rhy. Fig. 2   **End Rhy. Fig. 2**

Love   comes   o - ver   you.   Yes it does.

Gtr. 2: w/ Rhy. Fig. 2, 6 times, simile

Love   comes   o - ver   you.

WALKIN' BLUES
Words and Music by Robert Johnson

Figure 19 – Intro

"Walkin' Blues" is Eric's heartfelt homage to an original hero—Delta bluesman Robert Johnson. Johnson had been an influence on Clapton way before E.C. made his name a rock 'n' roll buzzword with his late-sixties rendition of "Crossroads" in Cream. Eric's interpretation here is very authentic and a virtual encyclopedia of country blues licks. He renders "Walkin' Blues" as an unaccompanied solo number with wistful vocals and a rootsy acoustic slide approach.

Clapton again plays his *Dobro in Open G tuning*—this time employing fingerstyle technique and harnessing its unmistakable guitar voice for a backporch, rural blues flavor. In fact, Clapton's version is a hybrid—grafting Robert Johnson's lyrics onto a guitar part borrowed from Muddy Waters's "Feel Like Going Home"—creating a simultaneous tribute to both of his early influences.

The intro employs a classic country blues dyad lick in characteristic triplet rhythm, implicit as the main pulse in the notated *12/8 time signature*. Measure 5 is an extra measure of 6/8, which transforms the piece into a *13-bar blues* structure. Note the reliance on chord-based sounds in measures 5–7. The slurred single-note and dyad licks in measures 8 and 9 are indispensable staples of the Delta style. The cadence figures in measures 10 and 11 outline the V–IV (D to C) chord change with a strong thematic motive incorporating a rising G arpeggio and slid notes which define the harmony (as either the fifth or fifth and root of the chord).

The *turnaround* in measures 12 and 13 is an emblematic cadence pattern found in countless blues tunes. Eric plays this part with fingered notes. It contains the G–G7–G6–G+5–G chord sequence formed by posing a descending chromatic line (the lowest notes on the fourth string) against constant G and B notes on the open third and second strings. Interestingly, this turnaround is found in many Robert Johnson songs including "Walkin' Blues," "Cross Road Blues," "Dead Shrimp Blues," and "Ramblin' On My Mind."

Fig. 19

39 **Featured Guitars:**
Gtr. 1 meas. 1-13

40 **Slow Demos:**
Gtr. 1 meas. 1-4;
5-9; 10-12

Open G Tuning:
① = D ④ = D
② = B ⑤ = G
③ = G ⑥ = D

* Played behind the beat.

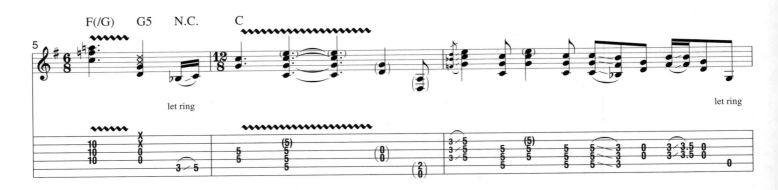

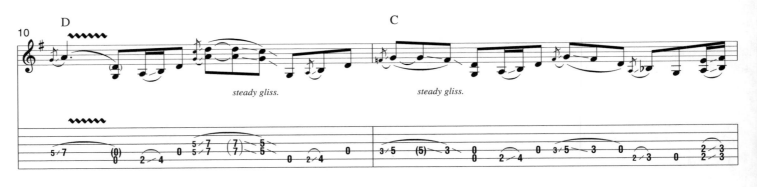

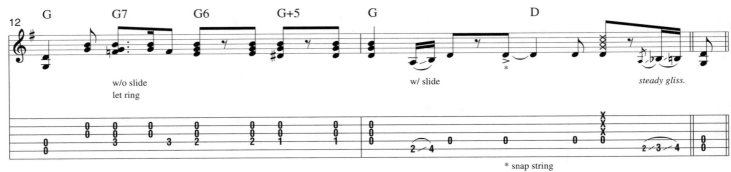

Figure 20 – Verse

In the verse, Clapton uses variation of the turnaround for the main I chord comping figure in measures 1–4. This alternates between fingered notes, the G7–G6–G chord progression, and a pickup (B♭–B) played with the slide bar. The IV-chord (C) sounds in measures 5 and 6 are all played with the slide and again exploit two- and three-note shapes that are easily accessed with the bar. In measures 7 and 8, Eric adds some arpeggio-based slide licks similar to those heard in the intro. The turnaround is recalled practically verbatim from the intro.

* Played behind the beat.

ALBERTA
New Words and New Music Adaptation by Huddie Ledbetter

Figure 21 – Intro and Verse

"Alberta" again looks back to Eric's distant past. The tune came to Clapton via New Orleans street musician Snooks Eaglin and the *Street Singer* album—both of which were highly influential to Eric as a beginning guitar player. Consisting of "three chords" and "just straight strumming," it was accessible to him at an early age, and also resonated as a very sentimental song. Eric later played this traditional country-blues tune during his 1976 and 1977 tours. On the *Unplugged* session, he used a 12-string acoustic and adhered to a simple, folk-inspired guitar approach.

"Alberta" is simple but not simpleminded. The song is built around three basic chords—C, F (occasionally Fm), and G—and utilizes straight eighth-note strumming patterns played with the pick. The eighth-note rhythms are set in a moderately-slow shuffle feel notated in 12/8 meter. Most of the strum patterns are grouped as three consecutive eighth notes to the beat or as a quarter-note-eighth-note figure.

In the intro, Eric adds connecting fills and counter melodies between the chords in measures 10–11 and 13–15. Note the hammer-on approach used in the intro in measures 10–13. On a 12-string these require a bit more left hand strength. The counter-melodies are thematic to the song and recur in successive verses as in measures 18, 22, and 27 of the first verse.

Featured Guitars:
Gtr. 1   meas. 1-27

Slow Demos:
Gtr. 1   meas. 3-7;
8-11; 12-15;
16-19; 20-26

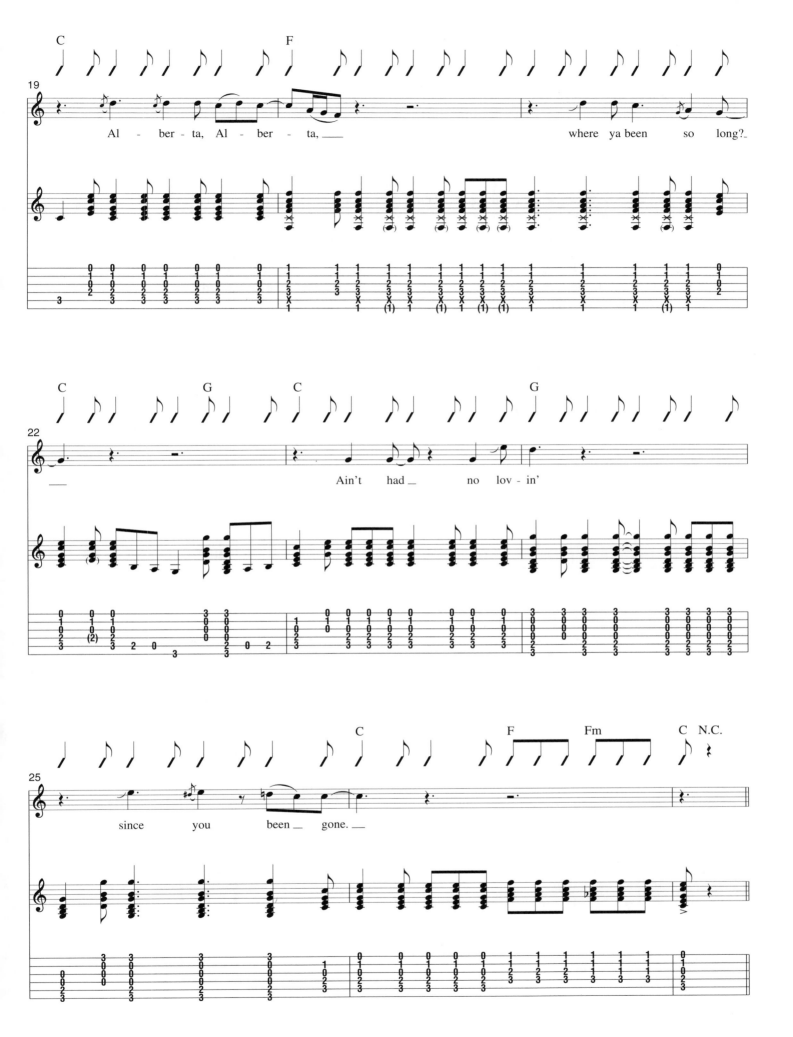

SAN FRANCISCO BAY BLUES

Words and Music by Jesse Fuller

Figure 22 – Verses 1 and 2

Another seminal influence on Clapton, "San Francisco Bay Blues" is attributed to folk & blues artist Jesse Fuller—a one-man band with a bank of invented instruments, two bass drums, a foot bass, harmonica, kazoos, and a 12-string guitar. In the *Unplugged* setting, this rousing uptempo shuffle is an ideal sing-along number and an undeniable catalyst for some enthusiastic audience participation. Appropriately, Eric performs it on 12-string acoustic and employs a folky, boisterous eighth-note strumming approach with the pick. The track also features a rare Eric Clapton kazoo solo. Andy Fairweather Low adds to the rollicking party mood with a wheezing harmonica solo and more propulsive strumming on his Gibson Super-400 arch top acoustic.

Like "Alberta," "San Francisco Bay Blues" is based on simple, first-position open chords: C, C7, A7, D7, G7 and E(7). The F chord used throughout is fingered like the C chord with the second and third fingers moved over one set of strings. The index finger barres the first and second strings in this voicing. Thumb fretting is used to play the F bass note in the chord as well as the F♯ bass note in the D7 chord of measures 13–14 and 29.

45 **Featured Guitars:**
Gtr. 1   meas. 1-32

46 **Slow Demos:**
Gtr. 1   meas. 1-8;
9-16; 17-24;
25-32

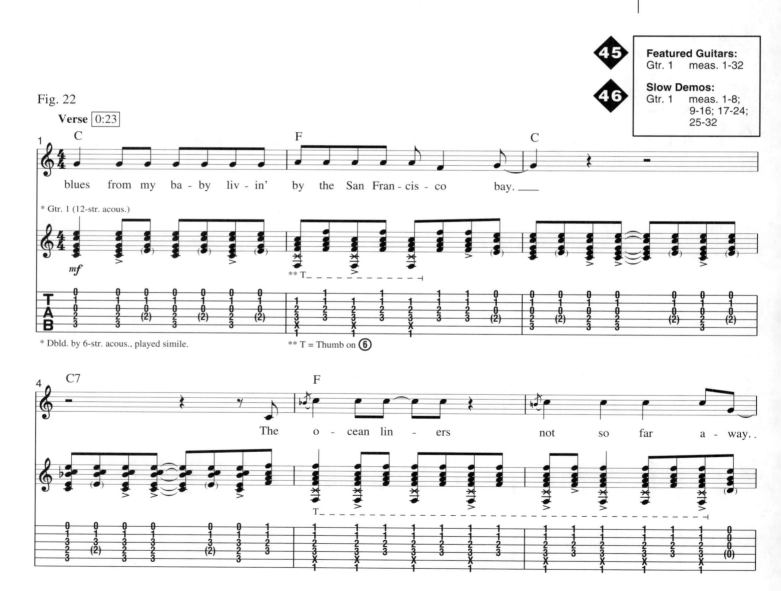

Fig. 22

* Dbld. by 6-str. acous., played simile.   ** T = Thumb on ⑥

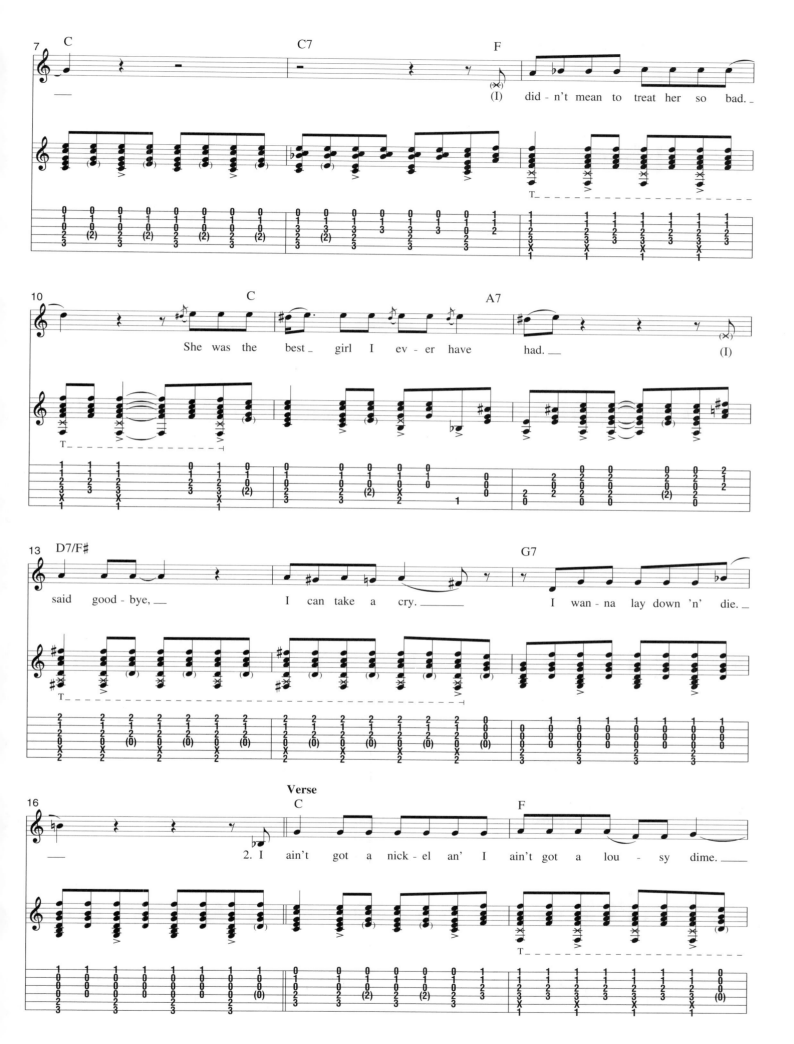

MALTED MILK
Words and Music by Robert Johnson

"Malted Milk" is the second Robert Johnson blues composition of the session and the closing number of the concert. For Clapton, its beauty and simplicity brought it all home. Clapton cites Johnson as his single most important influence, and approaches his music with care and respect. "Malted Milk" is no exception. This was a new piece in his repertoire, and it received a gorgeous, understated slow blues duet treatment with Andy Fairweather Low on second guitar. Both play subtle, but noteworthy, interlocking steel-string acoustic parts, creating an airy, introspective mood. The song is further distinguished by a particularly soulful Clapton vocal performance.

In the two-measure intro, both guitars paraphrase Robert Johnson's classic blues *turnaround figure*. Note the high E pedal tone on the first string with the chromatic descending bass counterpoint line implying the familiar progression E7–E6–E+–E/B.

The verse is a straight 12-bar blues in the key of E. Clapton takes the sparse, lower-register comping part—sticking primarily to the first position. For contrast, Low adds higher-register voicings, slurred seventh chords, single-note fills, and countermelody.

The closing cadence in measures 13 and 14 is a direct reference to Robert Johnson's original version and is unadulterated Delta eerieness. Here the progression is an unusual chromatic-seventh-chord sequence following the descending changes E–C♯7/G♯–C7/G–B7.

Fig. 23

Featured Guitars:
Gtr. 1   meas. 1-14

try'n to drive _ my blues a - way. _   I keep

drink - in' malt - ed milk _   try-in' to drive my _ blues a - way. _

Ba-by, you're just as wel-come to my lov-in' as the

grad. release

flow - ers is _____ in _ May. _

2. Malt - ed

Figure 24 – Guitar Solo

Clapton's solo is no less striking. An emotional and thematic moment, it occurs over one twelve-measure chorus of the blues in E. Eric plays it fingerstyle, with thumb, index, and middle fingers plucking notes and occasionally strumming chords as in measures 3-4 and 7-8. Note the sharp attacks in the solo, particularly in measures 1 and 4, attained by snapping the string against the fretboard.

The solo contains some trademark Slowhand scale *combining.* Note Eric's blend of E major pentatonic (E–F#–G#–B–C#), E Blues Scale (E–G–A–Bb–B–D) and E minor pentatonic (E–G–A–B–D) sounds throughout. The C# note figures prominently in measures 2, 5, 6, and 10, where it defines the major third of the A7 chord. The thematic melody figure in measures 2, 6 and 9-10, is comprised of an ascending arpeggio and descending chromatic notes, that blend the major pentatonic and blues scale. Note that it is a movable figure and is used against both A7 and B7 chords. The solo closes with a recall of the song's distinctive turnaround figure in measures 11 and 12.

48 Featured Guitars:
Gtr. 1   meas. 1-14

49 Slow Demos:
Gtr. 1   meas. 3-6;
7-10; 11-14

Fig. 24

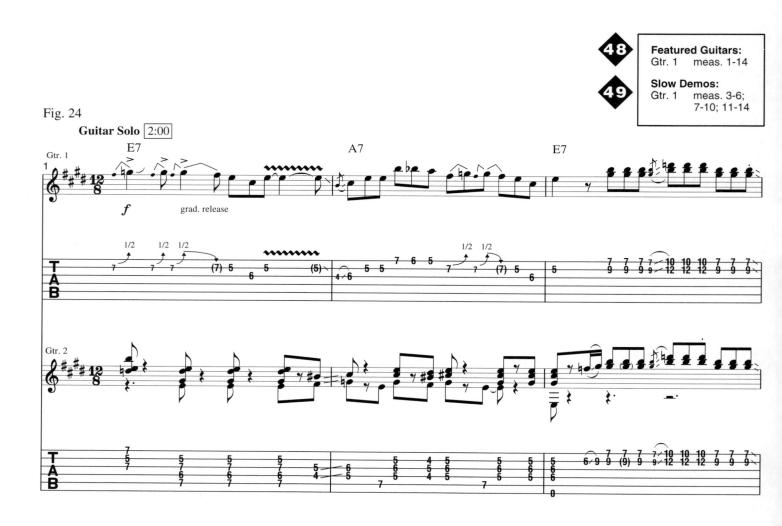

54

* snap string

4. My _ door

OLD LOVE
Words and Music by Eric Clapton and Robert Cray

Figure 25 – Intro, Verse, and Chorus

This remarkable live version of the popular Clapton track from *Journeyman* works beautifully in the setting of *Unplugged.* The moody song receives an atmospheric rock ballad treatment with supportive playing from the band, and features Eric and Andy picking and strumming on steel-string flat-top acoustics.

The tune is dominated by a strong modal riff in A minor introduced by Clapton as a solo intro in the opening measures. Played in the intro, verse, chorus, and behind the solo, it is built on a repeating two-measure, four-chord progression of Am–F/A–G7sus4–G. Note the use of partial-barre chord shapes on the top four strings with thumb-fretting on the sixth string throughout this figure. The intro riff's low-register pickup melody has clear allusions to "Layla" and is omitted from the more streamlined rhythm figure of the verse.

In measures 17–22, the progression moves through chords related to A minor. Note the use of F–E7 as well as Am–Am(maj7)–Am7–Am6 patterns in this section. Throughout these rhythm figures, Eric again employs thumb-fretting for the bass notes of the chords on the sixth string.

Featured Guitars:
Gtr. 1   meas. 1-26

Slow Demos:
Gtr. 1   meas. 1-4;
17-20; 21-24

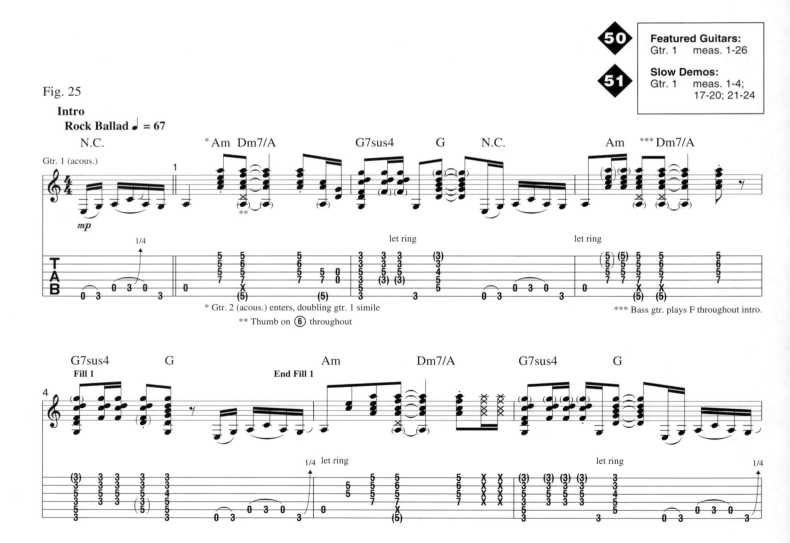

Fig. 25

Figure 26 – Guitar Solo

Eric's solo on "Old Love" is one of his most passionate. It is played with a flat pick and takes full advantage of the song's slow simmering groove to build a strong emotional statement. He conveys a flamboyant Gypsy flavor with flowing cascades of notes (often phrased rubato as in measures 3–4 and 11), ornamental trill figures (measures 2–5, 7, 12–14, 17–18, 20, and 23), and a general virtuosic attitude.

Clapton's lines are primarily diatonic single-note melodies, using the A natural minor scale (or Aeolian mode) (A–B–C–D–E–F–G). The occasional but expected foray into the A blues scale (A–C–D–E♭–E–G) is found in measures 5 and 16. To vary textures, Eric throws in double stops and chords in measures 1, 9, 15, and 22–23. These run the gamut from bent blues dyads to minor triads, parallel thirds, and dissonant major-second bursts.

Eric builds to a powerful mid-way climax in measures 12–13, with a driving ostinato figure reminiscent of his electric-blues style. A second strong climax is heard in the energetic scalar lines of measures 19–20. The solo comes to rest in measure 25 on a recap of the song's main riff.

Fig. 26

Guitar Solo

Featured Guitars:
Gtr. 1   meas. 1-28

Slow Demos:
Gtr. 1   meas. 1-24

* Played ahead of the beat.

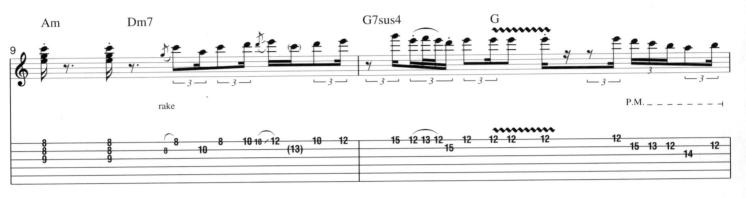

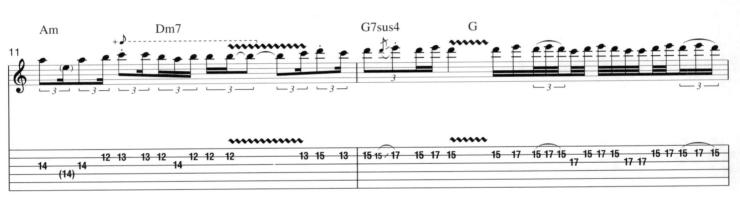

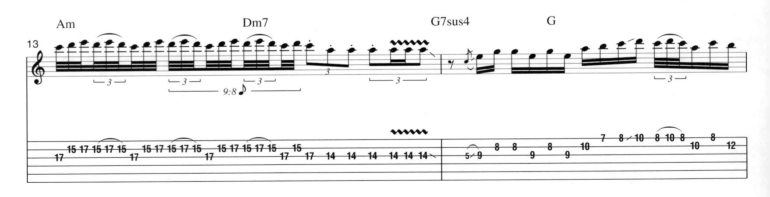

ROLLIN' AND TUMBLIN'
Written by Muddy Waters

Figure 27 – Verse and Guitar Solo

Muddy Waters's "Rollin' and Tumblin'" was originally recorded by Clapton in 1966 as part of the repertoire for *Fresh Cream*, and was a cornerstone of Cream's live set through the sixties. It was played as an ad lib break tune in the *Unplugged* session and became one of its many highlights. As the band fell into Clapton's insistent groove, an arrangement was created spontaneously, and the technicians shrewdly turned the recording equipment back on to capture the performance. The song was included as the final track of the *Unplugged* CD and video.

Eric plays "Rollin' And Tumblin'" as a slide guitar number on a Dobro in Open G tuning using a flat pick to strum chords and dyads, and to pick single note lines. Throughout, E.C. colors his playing with characteristic slurs and vibrato produced by the bottleneck.

The verse is an *altered blues* in G. Note that the section begins on the IV chord (C) but otherwise follows the standard blues form. The music is written in 2/4 meter so the measures must be combined to create a semblance of the 12-measure form. Other than the occasional extra 2/4 measures (measures 2, 11, 20, 29, 38, and 47), the structure is practically identical to the basic blues form with the same use of I, IV, and V chords, harmonic rhythm and overall proportions. This altered blues form is also found in the solo.

Throughout "Rollin' And Tumblin'," Clapton makes use of a motivic blues riff in G for the I chord of the progression. This main riff combines slurred dyads with single notes, and is based on the G minor pentatonic scale (G–B♭–C–D–F). Note the use of an ascending half-step slide into the B♭–D dyad during the riff (as in the pickup and measures 1, 8–10, 16–19, 25–28, etc.)—this figure recurs frequently throughout the song.

Eric takes a one-chorus solo at 0:46. He plays sparse single-note lines, basically paraphrasing the vocal melody over the C chord, but inevitably returns to the song's main riff between phrases for the G chord. This sets up the familiar call-and-response format of the blues in the body of the solo. In measures 48–51, Eric exploits chord sounds over the D and C progression. Due to the open tuning, these are easily performed as straight barre shapes with the slide.

Featured Guitars:
Gtr. 1   meas. 1-58

Slow Demos:
Gtr. 1   meas. 1-2;
2-11; 11-20;
21-29; 30-37;
38-47; 48-57

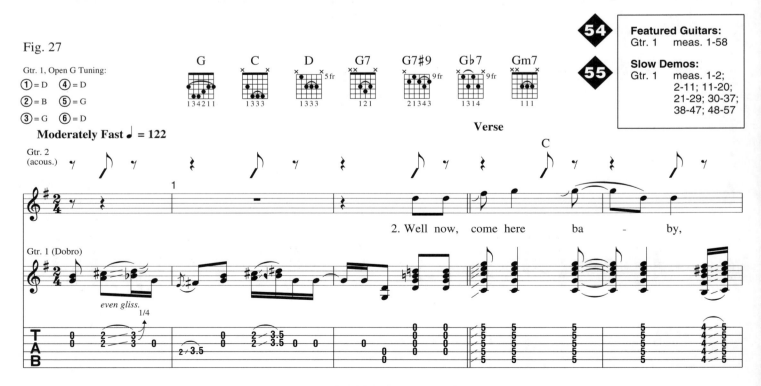

Fig. 27

I wan-na tell you a-bout ___ the ___ way ___ they treat-ed ___ me. ___

Guitar Solo

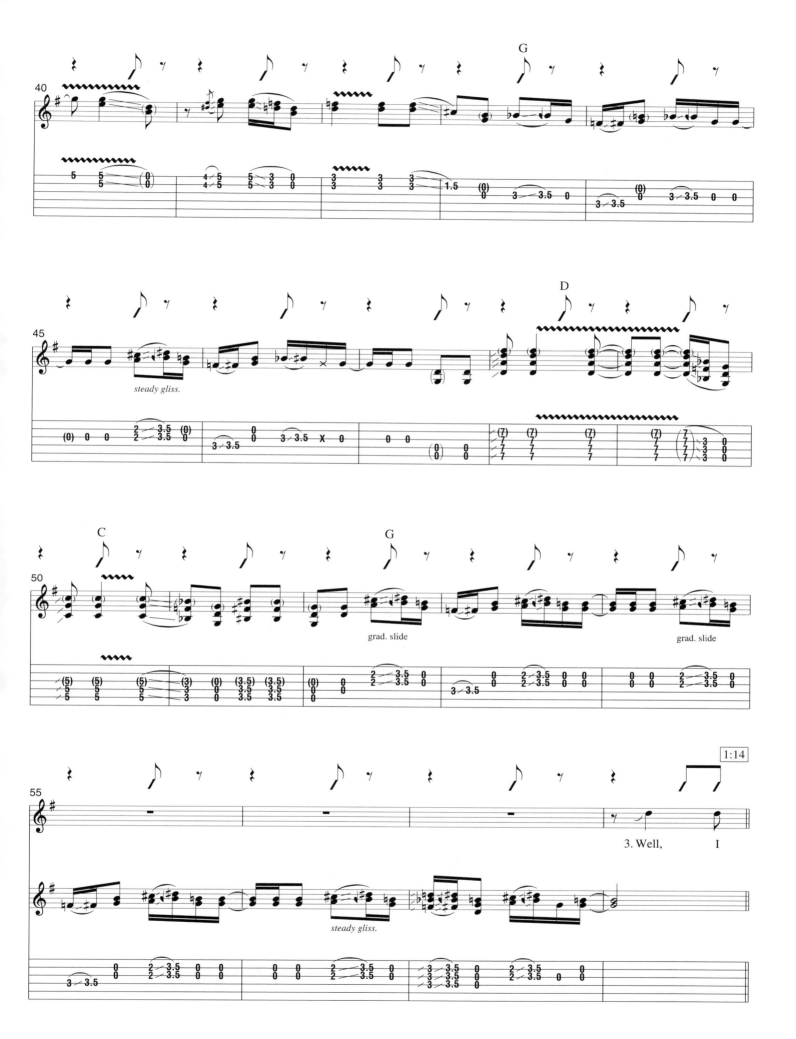

Figure 28 – Outro Guitar Solo

Eric's second solo (2:20) is played over a straight G vamp which boogies along with variants of the basic rhythm groove. Appropriately, Clapton begins with variations of the main riff in measures 9–30. In measures 31–38, he improvises slippery, single-note, chord based blues licks in G. Note the general use of G triads in this section—particularly the G major arpeggios in measures 33–34 and 39–42, and G7 arpeggio sounds in measures 37–38 and 43–46.

Clapton establishes a rousing, two-measure ostinato riff in measures 47–85 to build momentum in the outro. Note his subtle but deft variations of this ostinato riff with different double-stop, single-note and chord textures throughout—rarely are any of the two-measure patterns the same. The figure is again based on a G7 chord sound. Note the consistent use of the A–C♯ dyad to slide into the B♭–D dyad. The B♭ note in the riff emphasizes the minor/major/dominant harmonic ambiguity of blues music. The final whimsical blues lick in measure 94 (3:42) recalls the G major triad ideas heard earlier in the second solo.

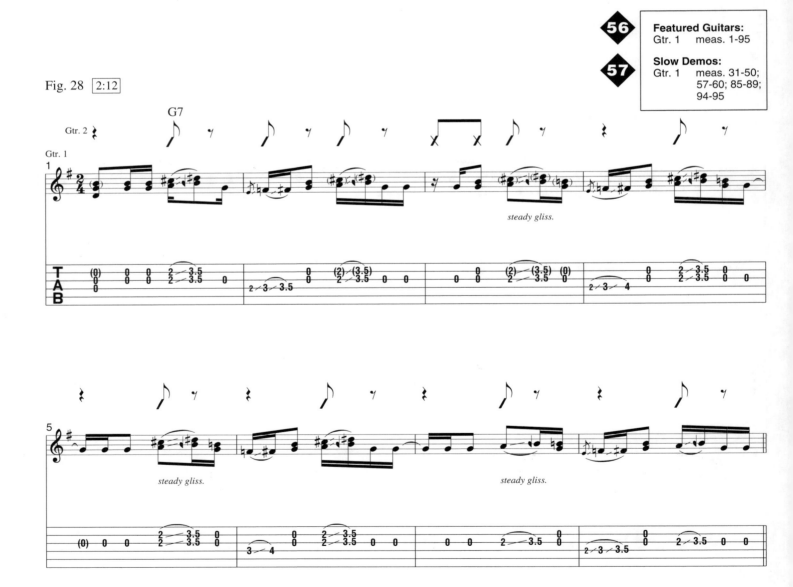

Fig. 28 2:12

Featured Guitars:
Gtr. 1   meas. 1-95

Slow Demos:
Gtr. 1   meas. 31-50;
57-60; 85-89;
94-95

Outro Guitar Solo 2:20

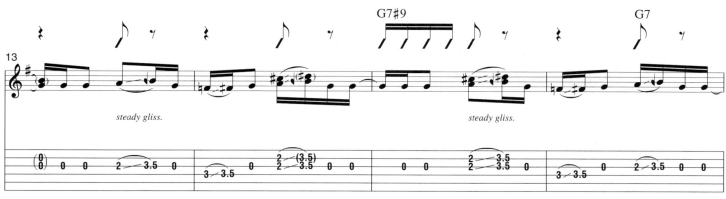

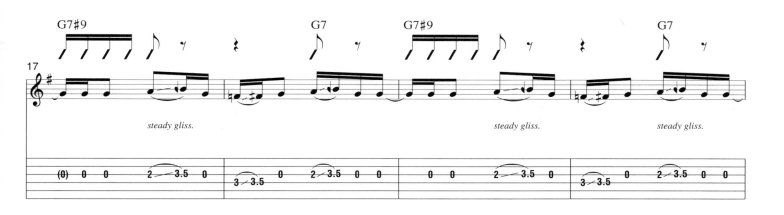

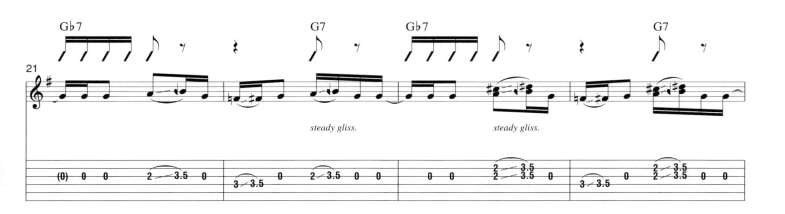

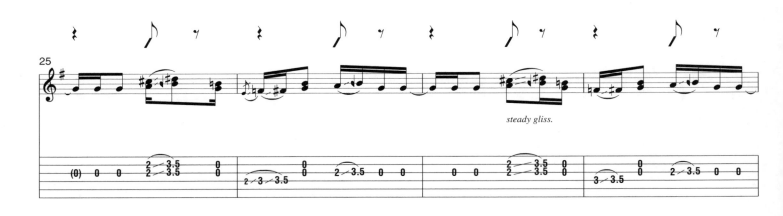

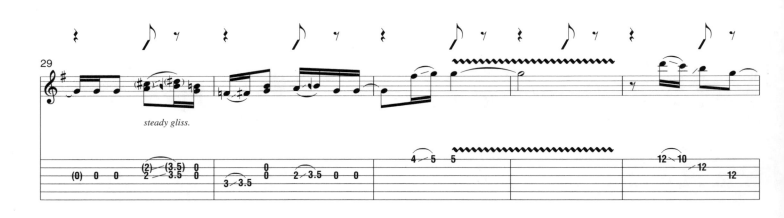

Gtr. 2: w/ Rhy. Fig. 1, 27 times

Gm7

Rhy. Fig. 1

End Rhy. Fig. 1

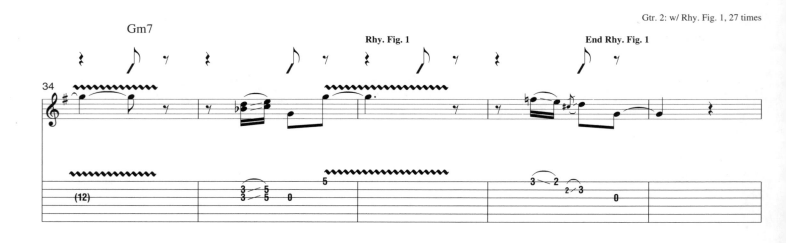

* slightly flat

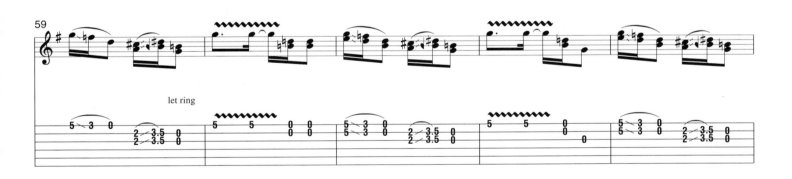

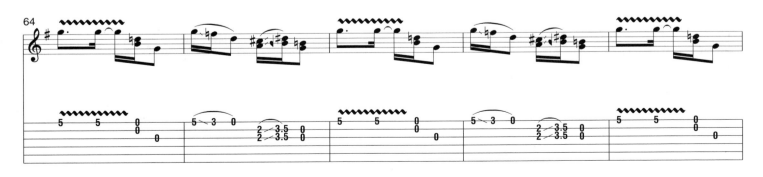

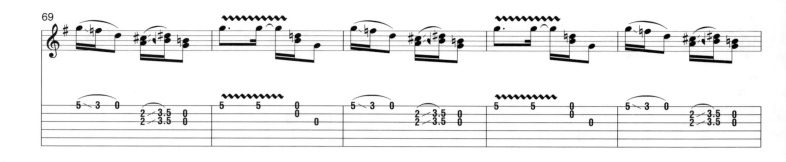

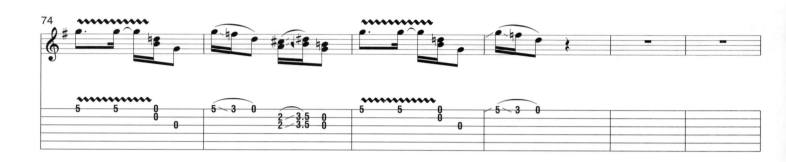

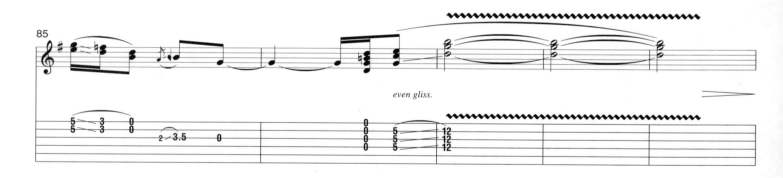

even gliss.

3:54

Gtr. 2 tacet

Gm7

Gtr. 2

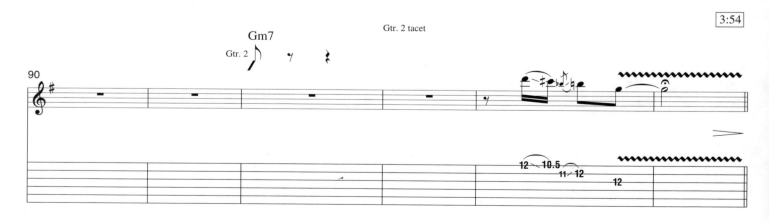

GUITAR NOTATION LEGEND

Guitar Music can be notated three different ways: on a *musical staff*, in *tablature*, and in *rhythm slashes*.

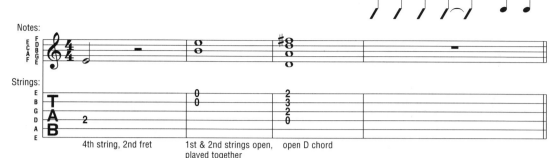

RHYTHM SLASHES are written above the staff. Strum chords in the rhythm indicated. Use the chord diagrams found at the top of the first page of the transcription for the appropriate chord voicings. Round noteheads indicate single notes.

THE MUSICAL STAFF shows pitches and rhythms and is divided by bar lines into measures. Pitches are named after the first seven letters of the alphabet.

TABLATURE graphically represents the guitar fingerboard. Each horizontal line represents a string, and each number represents a fret.

HALF-STEP BEND: Strike the note and bend up 1/2 step.

WHOLE-STEP BEND: Strike the note and bend up one step.

GRACE NOTE BEND: Strike the note and bend up as indicated. The first note does not take up any time.

SLIGHT (MICROTONE) BEND: Strike the note and bend up 1/4 step.

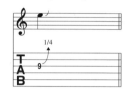

BEND AND RELEASE: Strike the note and bend up as indicated, then release back to the original note. Only the first note is struck.

PRE-BEND: Bend the note as indicated, then strike it.

VIBRATO: The string is vibrated by rapidly bending and releasing the note with the fretting hand.

WIDE VIBRATO: The pitch is varied to a greater degree by vibrating with the fretting hand.

HAMMER-ON: Strike the first (lower) note with one finger, then sound the higher note (on the same string) with another finger by fretting it without picking.

PULL-OFF: Place both fingers on the notes to be sounded. Strike the first note and without picking, pull the finger off to sound the second (lower) note.

LEGATO SLIDE: Strike the first note and then slide the same fret-hand finger up or down to the second note. The second note is not struck.

SHIFT SLIDE: Same as legato slide, except the second note is struck.

TRILL: Very rapidly alternate between the notes indicated by continuously hammering on and pulling off.

TAPPING: Hammer ("tap") the fret indicated with the pick-hand index or middle finger and pull off to the note fretted by the fret hand.

NATURAL HARMONIC: Strike the note while the fret-hand lightly touches the string directly over the fret indicated.

PINCH HARMONIC: The note is fretted normally and a harmonic is produced by adding the edge of the thumb or the tip of the index finger of the pick hand to the normal pick attack.

PICK SCRAPE: The edge of the pick is rubbed down (or up) the string, producing a scratchy sound.

MUFFLED STRINGS: A percussive sound is produced by laying the fret hand across the string(s) without depressing, and striking them with the pick hand.

PALM MUTING: The note is partially muted by the pick hand lightly touching the string(s) just before the bridge.

RAKE: Drag the pick across the strings indicated with a single motion.

TREMOLO PICKING: The note is picked as rapidly and continuously as possible.

VIBRATO BAR DIVE AND RETURN: The pitch of the note or chord is dropped a specified number of steps (in rhythm) then returned to the original pitch.

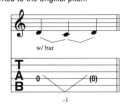

VIBRATO BAR SCOOP: Depress the bar just before striking the note, then quickly release the bar.

VIBRATO BAR DIP: Strike the note and then immediately drop a specified number of steps, then release back to the original pitch.

GUITAR *signature licks*

The Signature Licks book/audio packs are especially formatted to give you instruction on how to play a particular artist style by using the actual transcribed, "right from the record" licks! Designed for use by anyone from beginner right up to the experienced player who is looking to expand his insight. The books contain full performance notes and an overview of each artist or group's style with transcriptions in notes and tab. The audio features playing tips and techniques as well as playing examples at a slower tempo.

Acoustic Guitar Of '60s And '70s
by Wolf Marshall
A step-by-step breakdown of acoustic guitar styles and techniques featuring 14 classic rock examples, including: Here Comes The Sun • Fire And Rain • Dust In The Wind • Babe, I'm Gonna Leave You • Angie • and more.

00695024 Book/CD Pack.....................................$19.95

Acoustic Guitar Of '80s And '90s
by Wolf Marshall
Learn to play acoustic guitar in the styles and techniques of today's top performers. This book/CD pack features detailed instruction on 15 examples, including: Tears In Heaven • Patience • Losing My Religion • Wanted Dead Or Alive • and more.

00695033 Book/CD Pack.....................................$19.95

The Best Of Eric Clapton
by Jeff Perrin
A step-by-step breakdown of his playing technique through a hands-on analysis of classics. Includes: After Midnight • Crossroads • Layla • Tears In Heaven • Wonderful Tonight • and more.

00695038 Book/CD Pack.....................................$19.95

The Best Of Def Leppard
A step-by-step breakdown of the band's guitar styles and techniques featuring songs from four albums. The audio accompaniment presents each song in a stereo split with full band backing. Songs include: Bringin' On The Heartbreak • Hysteria • Photograph • and more.

00696516 Book/CD Pack.....................................$19.95

Jimi Hendrix
12 songs presented with all of the guitar parts fully transcribed, plus accompanying audio on CD, as performed by a full band. A performance notes, outlining chord voicings, scale use, and unusual techniques are including for each song. Songs include: Foxy Lady • Hey Joe • Little Wing • Purple Haze • and more.

00696560 Book/CD Pack.....................................$19.95

Eric Johnson
Learn the nuances of technique and taste that make Eric Johnson unique among guitarists. On this pack's 60-minute audio supplement, Wolf Marshall explores both the theoretical and hands-on aspects of Eric Johnson's best recorded work. It also comprehensively explores: Hybrid picking • String-skipping • Motivic development • Scale-combining • Position shifting • and additional aspects of his playing that makes him one of the most admired guitarists today. Some of his best songs are examined, including: Trademark • Cliffs Of Dover • Song For George • and more.
00699317 Book/CD Pack $19.95
00699318 Book/Cassette Pack.............................$17.95

The Best Of Kiss
Learn the trademark riffs and solos behind one of rock's most legendary bands. This pack includes a hands-on analysis of 12 power house classics, including: Deuce • Strutter • Rock And Roll All Nite • Detroit Rock City • and more.

00699412 Book/Cassette Pack.........................$17.95
00699413 Book/CD Pack.................................$19.95

The Guitars Of Elvis
by Wolf Marshall
Elvis' music is synonymous with the birth of rock and roll and the invention of rock guitar. Wolf Marshall takes you back to the roots where it all started with this exploration into the influential style of the King's fretmen. This book is a step-by-step breakdown of the playing techniques of Scotty Moore, Hank Garland, and James Burton. Players will learn their unique concepts and techniques by studying this special collection of Elvis' greatest guitar-driven moments. The 75-minute accompanying audio presents each song in stereo-split with full band backing. Songs include: A Big Hunk O' Love • Heartbreak Hotel • Hound Dog • Jailhouse Rock • See See Rider • and more!
00696508 Book/Cassette Pack............................$17.95
00696507 Book/CD Pack $19.95

Rolling Stones
by Wolf Marshall
A step-by-step breakdown of the guitar styles of Keith Richards, Brian Jones, Mick Taylor and Ron Wood. 17 songs are explored, including: Beast Of Burden • It's Only Rock 'n' Roll (But I Like It) • Not Fade Away • Start Me Up • Tumbling Dice • and more.

00695079 Book/CD Pack.....................................$19.95

Best Of Carlos Santana
Explore the music behind one of the guitar's greatest innovators. A Hands-on analysis of 13 classics, including Black Magic Woman • Evil Ways • Oye Como Va • Song Of The Wind • and more.

00695010 Book/CD Pack.....................................$19.95

Steve Vai
Play along with the actual backing tracks from *Passion and Warfare* and *Sex and Religion* especially modified by Steve Vai himself! Learn the secrets behind a guitar virtuoso then play along like the pro himself.

00673247 Book/CD Pack.....................................$22.95

Stevie Ray Vaughan
by Wolf Marshall
This book takes you on an in-depth exploration of this guitar genius by examining various aspects of Vaughan's playing. Marshall explains his influences, tuning, equipment, picking technique and other aspects of Vaughan's sound. In addition, he transcribes, in notes and tab, parts of 13 of Vaughan's most famous songs, and explains how they were played and what makes them so unique. The 59-minute accompanying cassette or CD includes samples of the parts of the songs being examined. A must for any serious Vaughan fan or aspiring guitarist!
00699315 Book/Cassette Pack............................$17.95
00699316 Book/CD Pack $19.95

Prices, contents, and availability subject to change without notice. Some products may not be available outside the U.S.A.

FOR MORE INFORMATION, SEE YOUR LOCAL MUSIC DEALER, OR WRITE TO:

HAL•LEONARD™
CORPORATION
7777 W. BLUEMOUND RD. P.O. BOX 13819 MILWAUKEE, WI 53213

http://www.halleonard.com

0298